Swingin' Loose

Swingin' Loose

Inside & Outside

Jane Lee Wolfe

White River Press
Amherst, Massachusetts

Swingin' Loose
Jane Lee Wolfe

Copyright 2013 © Jane Lee Wolfe

Book and cover design:
Douglas Lufkin, Lufkin Graphic Designs

Cover photo:
The Beach Lodge, Port Aransas, Texas
by Barry Amer, Barry Amer Photography

White River Press
PO Box 3561
Amherst, MA 01004
www.whiteriverpress.com

ISBN 978-1-935052-66-1

Library of Congress Cataloging-in-Publication Data

Wolfe, Jane Lee, 1939-
    Swingin' loose : inside & outside / Jane Lee Wolfe.
    pages cm
    ISBN 978-1-935052-66-1 (pbk. : alk. paper)
1. Christian life. 2. Spirituality--Christianity. I. Title.
BV4501.3.W6515 2013
248.4--dc23
                        2013024349

Dedication

The writing is for everyone, but *Swingin' Loose* is dedicated to women inside prison. Women inside prison are as under-served as they are in the outside world. So this is for you, ladies, as we make our way forward, inside and outside!

About Swingin' Loose Writings

This book could be called "Hey, Everybody," because every month I write a letter to "Hey, Everybody" about whatever seems best to talk about spiritually—at the moment. *Swingin' Loose* is a couple of years of those letters—maybe more. I'm still writing them every month.

There appears to be no overall order to the subject matter, even to me. In a way this reflects the way we develop spiritually—a little insight about one thing, followed by a little insight about another, then another—all seemingly unrelated. After a while though, the combined insights work together to build the spirit's endurance and make it both stronger and more flexible.

In this way it is kind of like body work—all over the place: you stretch your muscles, tone your core, increase the flexibility of your spine, clean up your food and beverage intake, etc. As you keep working at it, it all comes together for better health and better fitness. You not only feel better, you ARE better. You swing looser!

Have a good time with these letters. They are written to you, wherever you are, however you feel, whatever is or isn't going on in your life. Together—you reading, me writing—we are prepping for the present. It may not seem like we're doing much; but I guarantee you, it's awesome: building a powerful and healthy spirit to face each day—inside and outside.

Blessings,
Jane

Contents

Swingin' Loose

New Year Resolution Time

Hey, what is God's New Year Resolution? Short answer: who knows? Longer answer: Well, God has a track record of being interested in the following:

Peace	**Love**	**Poor**
Justice	**Humility**	**Thanksgiving**
Joy	**Blessings**	**Needy**
Kindness	**Praise**	**Forgiveness**
Healing	**Cleansing**	**Etc.**

It would be good if each of us helped God out by picking one of these things and made a point of working it from two angles—receiving and giving. It would be even better if we presented the list to God and said, "Which of these is mine for working on this year, for receiving and giving?"

Could be you would hear "Etc." in which case you would have to listen further to hear what the "Etc." was. But it could be that you would hear one of the other things on the list.

Here's the question: Have any of us got the nerve to listen to God say "Peace"? Here's a helping tip: If God says something scary and difficult like Peace or Justice, God will inform you what that means for you. The only deal is that you have to keep listening throughout the year. God rarely lays out a whole big plan for the year with instructions for following it. It's much more of a step-by-step, day-by-day kind of plan. And some days there is nothing, which is kind of your days off.

Next tip: God is never going to give you a daily plan that you can't accomplish. God is well aware of your situation. If you are handicapped and ancient, God is not going to suggest you participate in a Race for the Cure though you may be a companion for breast cancer victims, able to give them a warm hand, a smile, or a letter of caring in the mail.

See? So a good resolution would be to chance opening your heart to listen to God and what God has in mind for you. You will be pleased and surprised and filled with joy, for God loves us working together with him, happily and in harmony.

Gifts vs. Call

It is interesting to know what your gifts are, and there are some excellent workshops that can be offered to help you discover your gifts if you don't know them. These workshops are always fun too—several days all about me!

More relevant and closer to the power and dynamic of the gospel, however, is the business of call. Call is a response to God and your relationship with God. Call may or may not engage your gifts, but call is what you are obedient to whether or not your gifts are engaged.

Call comes from God, from Christ. If we listen, we find we are called to all sorts of things. Some of these engage our gifts, skills or expertise, and some do not.

We must always listen for and to call. Sometimes call is glorious and fun—David dancing naked before the ark—and sometimes call is tiresome and difficult— Moses called to lead the people of Israel out of Egypt and to the Promised land when he himself had a speech defect and had to have his brother Aaron do the talking for him. Hard call. Well met. Obedient to the relationship with God.

It is well to take your gifts seriously and to consider them holy offerings to God and God's people. That is what they are. But they are never more important than your calls.

Listen for your calls. Calls will take you places you never dreamed of, places God has arranged for you to be, places that will bring you joy no matter how easy or how difficult. Call leads us as we are to the place we are supposed to be. In the process of following our call, we are transformed, becoming the people God calls us to be.

Lent coming up? How about listening. How about listening to how much you are loved. How about listening to how God enjoys spending time with you. How about listening to what God has planned for the two of you. Lent is a good time for listening, a quiet time when call can be heard in the heart and following begun, holding the hand of Christ.

Confessing Your Blessings

We get pretty good at confessing our sins since we do it all the time. But how good are we at confessing the things that are good about ourselves, the things we've done right, the contributions we've made to someone's self-concept, the things we can say "yes!" to about ourselves, our relationships with others and with God.

This is something we need to do. The fact is, you can't get it wrong every time—you just aren't that bad. So what about taking some regular time to articulate the things you do well regularly, or even unexpectedly! You can take a confession of sin and turn it into a confession of blessing:

Most Glorious God, we rejoice that you have blessed us in thought and word and deed, and have blessed those things we have done and left undone. We have loved you with our whole heart, and we have loved our neighbors as ourselves. We joyfully accept your blessings and are wholeheartedly grateful for them. With Jesus and all your saints, let us celebrate and live boldly with the gifts and blessings you have given us. We delight in your will, we walk in your ways, in the glory of your name, and in the majesty of the goodness with which you have created us. Amen.

Then you can mediate on the following blessings:

- What is great about my body?

- What is great about my mind?

- What is great about my spirit?

- What is something I have not done that I am proud of not doing?

- What is something I have done that I am proud of doing?

- What is great about me in my relationships with other people?

- What is great about me in my relationship with God?

You can end your meditation with a different Confession of Blessings:

Holy God, we have got it right and followed your voice like sheep, happy in the companionship of each other and with you. We have followed your voice and listened to the desires of your heart. We have been obedient to our relationship with you and have rejoiced in the responsibilities and rights that have flowed for this relationship. We have allowed you to keep us from behaviors that would be harmful to others, to ourselves and to you. We have responded to your call and have acted in ways that have enabled us and others to live holy lives that glorify you. You have blessed us, you have rejoiced in our love of you, or love of each other and our love of ourselves. You have given us growth and maturity. You have taught us to celebrate our blessings. You have enabled us to live your promises of wholeness as Christ Jesus lived his. Thank you for bestowing on us blessings of body, mind and spirit, and for allowing us to praise your glory. Amen.

Prayer Crafting

Most of us have personal prayers that we offer God on a regular and on a situational basis. Most of these are petitions—asks—for one thing or another. These asks need not be selfish, they can be for peace, justice, an end to war and hunger—anything. They also can address your personal life, your family, your hopes and fears, etc.

Petitions are the most common form of prayer, even in *The Book of Common Prayer* sitting in your pew or on your bedside table or in your library. However, petition is not the only form of prayer and often not the most important form.

The most important form of a prayer is the one that has power for you. If petition seems boring or meaningless, try changing a familiar prayer, personal or in *The Prayer Book*, into another form. Here are some suggestions:

Listen the prayer

> *I am your Father in Heaven, my name is Holy, my Kingdom comes, my will is done on earth and in heaven. I feed you, I forgive you and you forgive others. I keep You from temptation and deliver you from evil.*

Thank the prayer

> *I thank you Father in Heaven, I thank you that you are Holy, that your kingdom comes and your will is done...*

Praise the prayer

I praise you, Father in Heaven, I praise your holy name, I praise your kingdom and your will. I praise you for...

Believe

I believe that you are my father in heaven, that your Name is holy, that your kingdom comes...

There are so many ways that you can transform a prayer into a state other than petition. Again, the point is to find the form that has power for you, that day.

The listening form is often the most powerful. It allows us to hear God speak to us instead of us continually speaking to God. In a world confused and suffering, it is reassuring, ennobling and empowering to hear God speak with power and love. Take the Prayer attributed to St. Francis:

I am the instrument of your peace. Where there is hatred, I sow love; where there is injury, I pardon; where there is discord, I unite; where there is doubt, I bring faith; where there is despair, I give hope; where there is darkness, I give light; where there is sadness, I bring joy. I console you, I understand you, I love you. I give to you and you receive; I pardon and you pardon; and I bring you to eternal life when you die. Amen.

Greetings!

"Greetings!" This is how Jesus starts off the day on Easter Sunday according to Matthew.

Will you look at all that! He doesn't say "Boy, I had a really hard time but thank goodness it's over," or anything like that. He just says the equivalent of "Hi!"

The Resurrection Jesus is a fabulous and fabulously different individual from the pre-resurrection person. This is never discussed at much length; people are too tired from being serious and sincere throughout Lent to have much interest in anything other than "Whew! Glad that's over!"

In a couple of Gospels, Easter Jesus gets after them a little bit and in one he does a bit of teaching while on a hiking trip that goes through Emmaus, but in general he is soft and pleasant and different. He is resurrected, he is ascending to the father, and he is living the life he has been calling us to right along. He models Resurrection behavior for us to live. Of all times in the liturgical year, this is the most important for those of us who need some clear "how to's" for healthy spiritual living.

Model #1: When he gets to some place he says "Greetings!" or "Peace be with you!" He's all about peace, that peace he talks about before he dies when he says "My peace I give to you, my peace I leave with you." Well, he's left it with us and he takes advantage of it himself. His personality and person are awash in peace. Peace be with you, every day, every time.

Model #2: When he is hungry he asks for something to eat and he cooks for those who are hungry.

Model #3: He's fully into the present. He doesn't talk about the past and makes no mention of the future. He lives whole and soft and comfortable in the present.

Model #4: He asks questions but ones he knows the answers to and he's pleasant about them—"Caught any fish? Need to see me to believe?"

Model #5: He's given up on being frustrated. He's relaxed, he's fun, and he's genial.

All this good stuff! It is so uplifting, so fun, so fine, and so full of grace! Remember when he died everyone was sad? Well, look at their response to Resurrection Jesus when he goes away for good this time: they return home filled with joy!

The moral: Wherever you go say "Greetings" or "Peace;" eat when you're hungry, cook when you feel like it, offer a little insight here and there, stop being frustrated, relax. This is the resurrected life, free from want and judgment, filled with rest and joy. It transforms you, and it transforms others in your presence.

Well done, good and faithful servant!

Now isn't that a nice thing for Jesus to say? We think so. We think somehow, too, that it is reachable for us—there's the off chance that Jesus would say something like that to us. We might not be able to respond "send me" to some scary-sounding assignment like prophesying to the world, but there is probably some domestic or social task we could do with which God would be well pleased.

And of course this is true. But we fail to hear Jesus say this to us a lot of the time. We have done a bunch of good deeds and we are pretty sure they are in line with something God would want us to do, but we don't have Jesus come and plop down beside us and say, "Well done, good and faithful servant." Why do you suppose that is?

The reason for so few heavenly compliments in response to our good works springs from this: we are not paying attention to what it takes to be a good servant.

What is the first quality of a good servant? The servant listens to what the boss has in mind. The good servant doesn't "figure" what the boss has in mind, the good servant doesn't come up with surprise good works without having a clue what kind of things please the boss. The good servant first and foremost lives in respectful relationship with the boss, listening, learning the boss's pleasure, fulfilling the tasks assigned, taking a day off when assigned.

That doesn't mean there is no place for creativity and surprise. It does mean, however, you have to be working the relationship smoothly first and within that the space for your own genius and gift show up. But you have to learn the relationship first. You have to develop a strong, flexible, trusting relationship. Then you can dance through the job.

Of course there are good things we do. But if we want to be good servants and not just random doers of good, we need to listen to the boss, let that relationship develop, get to know each other and go forth as instructed, checking in to see if we are on course with the job. This is not scary, and it's not even tiresome. Believe it or not, God generally wants less "work" than we are prepared to give. God enjoys just sitting around with us and being happy.

Fancy that, having a good rest for days on end and having Jesus say, "Well done, good and faithful servant!"

Conversations

Me: "His name is George."
My Mother: "No, his name is Bill."
Me: "No, he's my friend, and I know his name is George."
My Mother: "Well it should be Bill. He looks like a Bill."

Conversations like this are just wonderful. Completely nutty, they point to the fact that the search for accuracy and information is clearly no match for the desire to preserve our own world view down to the least detail.

When it involves George and/or Bill, we get it. When it involves God, other human beings and the planet, we're not so sure. In fact, we are pretty sure his name is Bill, no matter what God says about George and the rest. The world looks like a Bill—because Bill is our world, the one we like, the one we live in, the one we can cope with.

George's world is scary. Bad things happen. People suffer. The planet is torn apart and trashed. Things don't get better. Nothing seems to get fixed. God and George's world is depressing. Let's think about Bill and his world and maybe everything will be all right. We can say a prayer for George on Sunday and hope God turns him into Bill. George would like to be Bill, we know that.

This nonsense happens for several reasons:

1. We have not been taught how to experience the enormous protection with which God embraces us in the world called George, or how to experience God's enfolding love of us as we partner together in the

powerful experience of greeting the human race and the planet face to face.

2. We are raised on reportage of enormous sadness and things going wrong while there are many, many instances of peace, grace, and glory. Peace, grace, and glory don't build fear, though, and fear is the most effective way to manipulate people on anything from absurd to dangerous: from fear that you won't have the right clothes for an event to fear that there will be no food, water, shelter or clothing in the days to come.

3. We have not been raised to understand that our job is to "help" not "fix it." And help in companionship with God. The "help" may fail or not be enough, but "help" is the call, not "fix it."

Solutions? How to learn to live and thrive in a world called George? A few:

1. Let God set the threshold—let your heart be opened to care and help, knowing that you will be loved and protected and that an Olympic sized ball of suffering will not be thrown your way.

2. Don't take charge, but hold God's hand all the way.

3. Don't worry about not seeing the results. This is necessary in developing a "help" way of living and knowing and serving effectively.

4. Thank God each day for the protection, love and holding hands.

5. Enjoy the relationship, out of which flows blessed things and peace to a world called George.

Summer for the Soul

A few spiritual health basics to get you through the summer.

1. Show up. It's not about you OR God; it's about relationship—YOU AND GOD. You are not "here" and God "there;" the two of you are together. Just like any relationship, you have to show up for it. Showing up for your partner God is 90% of what it takes to be spiritually healthy.

2. Listen to your partner. Don't go "figuring" what God would like or enjoy or be proud of—listen. Mostly you'll find that God likes to just sit around and be with you.

3. Don't mix up public and personal persona. You are slightly different in public than you are in private and so is God. If you just keep with "church" God—king of kings, savior of the world, etc., you'll find God startlingly unresponsive on a personal level. That's the public God; learn the one who hangs around with you.

4. Don't get frantic about "good works." They're "gooder" if you do them with your partner than if you just tick them off solo.

5. Let life slow down internally. When you let God shoulder a good part of your life and concerns,

you feel rested. You may be busy on the outside, but since God is in charge of the burdens, you are lighter—less frantic.

6. Know that your relationship with God is the greatest gift you can accept for yourself and give to the world.

7. Throw worry and anger and fear in the garbage and let angels take them to the curb for heavenly trash pick up. Say thank you for this daily service.

8. Remember that spiritual health is a matter of daily pleasure and daily return to relationship with God.

9. Enjoy your partner and enjoy yourself. Let God enjoy God's partner and Godself.

10. Yeah!

God Manners

You know, it's a funny thing, but a lot of the time we treat God a good bit worse than we'd treat another human being. On the plus side (if there is one), God can probably take it; on the minus side, being rude, sloppy and disrespectful must make it hard for God to get a kick out of the relationship with us even if God's love never waivers.

Consider this: When was the last time you asked God about the day? "Hi, how was your day?" I went over 30 years without asking this question and I'm in the relationship-with-God business! How dumb can you get? And even if God just says "fine," well, at least you asked and listened for an answer. We rarely do this, ask or listen.

Then we tend to walk into church or some place where we honor our relationship with God in some kind of way, and bark out a few requests as though God was a supernatural waiter—rain please, less humidity please, more cash please, fix the Gulf oil spill, stop war, take care of Mary, etc. etc.

There's nothing wrong with these requests, it's just that the conversation is entirely one sided—we sure don't hang around to listen to God bark out requests of us. Does God bark? We do get a little pastoral and liturgical reassurance that God loves us and hears our prayers, but we are pretty generally short on the experience of reassurance that comes from listening to God talk to us.

"Hi!" "How are you?" "How's it been going?" These are good questions to ask your family and friends, and good questions to ask God. And just as with your family and friends, it's good to listen to the answers. If this seems new and strange, here's what you do: Tune in with your heart, let it open. Listen. God's not going to talk your heart off right away, if ever. But I can assure you God will be pleased. Pleased to be inquired after, pleased to say "fine" or something, pleased to know one of the little ones is making time so that the two of them can sit together smiling and rest a while.

Construction Vehicle: Do Not Follow

"One of the best signs ever!" we think, as we are barreling down the highway following the Do Not Follow vehicle. Time passes, we head off on our own, leaving our place behind Do Not Follow to some other driver who will also love the big orange placard on the back of the big black truck.

Now let us come to one of Jesus' most frequent statements to the folks surrounding him: "Follow Me!" This comes up both before and after his death and resurrection. Must be important, right? Conservative answer: probably. Next question: So how are we doing with this big biblical placard: Following? Not Following? Don't Know? Hope So?

Look at this: We know where we are in relationship to the Do Not Follow vehicle. But in relationship to the Follow Me vehicle? We are pretty unclear. If we got on the automotive highway with that lack of clarity, we would be considered unsafe drivers, and chances are we would be a danger to ourselves and others. The funny part of coming upon the Do Not Follow vehicle comes from the fact that we can read and understand, and are just for the moment and in spite of ourselves, being a little "disobedient." A little wicked fun!

Follow Me. Believe you me; if a big truck has a big sign, a big spiritual leader has a big sign too. Follow me.

What would this mean? It means that LIFE WOULD BE A LOT EASIER FOR US. Have you ever gotten tired on the highway, tired of choices on what to do when, and simply followed a very good driver, maintaining his/her speed, passing when he/she passes, slowing up when he/she does the same?

That is what it is like if you follow Jesus. You don't have to do so much thinking or "figuring out" on your own. You follow. It is restful. It's not quite like Greyhound's "Leave the Driving to Us," but it's pretty close. Speed up here, slow down here, rest here. Nice. So how do you follow Jesus? First, you have to sit back and listen, look with your heart. See the sign. The sign is posted on the Presence that keeps your heart open and alert. Sometimes you know the person as Christ and sometimes, like the disciples after the resurrection, it takes your heart a while to figure it out. But the Follow Me person is there; that is the promise.

There are other people on the highway, but you don't have to pay them much mind, just the way, if you are following a good driver, you don't have to pay other drivers much mind—you are following the best. Sometimes you will go fast and sometimes you will go slow, sometimes you will rest. Occasionally you have a little wicked fun and do something different like follow the Do Not Follow sign, but you can always come back to the Follow Me vehicle, because it is always there.

Take a look. Follow Me. There it is right ahead of you. Get in lane behind the sign. Follow the Christ. Stop trying so hard yourself. Let the good driver take you where you want to go and take you the safest way to get there. Relax. Stop thinking. Just follow.

Mercy

Here's a word we don't use too much. Chances are we don't even really know what it means. A religious word, it doesn't figure in our everyday secular vocabulary. Lord, have mercy. What does that mean? We hardly know.

It's okay that we don't really know what it means, but in contemporary usage, it means kindness—with understanding, compassion and commitment thrown in. HOWEVER, why don't we just use "kindness" to get a better sense of the meaning: Lord, have mercy: Lord, be kind. We have a sense of what that means, and we are grateful. Kind is good. Kind is something we can be.

This is much easier than "mercy." Mercy sounds kind of stuck up: "I was merciful to the person in the park." "I was kind to the person in the park" sounds better. Of course we would never say either of these things out loud, because we've been brought up to never say "Yes!" to any of the good stuff, only to say "My bad!" to the bad stuff, followed by "Lord, have mercy; Lord, be kind." In our culture, it is perfectly okay to say "I was unkind," but totally not okay to say "I was kind/I was merciful."

So, here's the deal for the year coming up: How about contributing to a massive culture change and a massive contribution to the kindness of this world? How about learning to identify your ability to drink in joy and reach out in kindness? How about saying occasionally, first to yourself and then to others, "I was kind today. I did a kind thing."

Heretical? Culturally, yes; spiritually, no. To admit to positive acts of kindness is not to be arrogant. Quite the opposite, it is absolutely humble. How so? True kindness to another is a response to the joy within you. It is not the exercise of an obligation or a duty; it is not manipulative, calculating or "righteous." It is your holy heart reaching out to another. It is a heart smile, a heart touch, a heart embrace, a heart whisper that says "I know you, my sister, my brother, and I am glad we are together if only for an instant."

This will take courage and practice. We are well trained to be pitiful, poorly trained to be brothers and sisters who serve each other with gladness, confidence and joy. What a New Year's resolution: to be kind and to admit to it. We'll never have a kind world without your help; we'll never have a kind world without your coming out of the closet and saying, "Yes, Lord, today I was kind." Try it. You won't drop dead, and God has seen everything so if you bungle it, so what? Get up and try again.

Let's take a go at a kind world. Let's take a go at saying, "Thank you, Lord, for letting me be kind." Let's take a go at standing up for the great and holy people God has created us to be. Don't worry, you'll have plenty of opportunity to be pitiful; but don't let the pity-you rain on your kind self. Thank you, Lord, as I live kindly in this world!

Mary, Joseph & Baby Jesus, etc.

Who are these people? A teenaged mom, an older man who hears voices, a baby arriving while on a medically unwise journey for census purposes? These are not people we commonly admire in real life, yet because they are long ago and far away and have gotten some unbelievably positive press over the years, we smile and think they're the best. And maybe they are the best; but we need to know this from experience, not just from the press, if our faith is to have legs to walk on and food to thrive by in our current world.

There are many ways to experience Mary, Joe and Jees (as a child friend called him). As the hymn says, "we can meet them in schools, or in lanes or at tea... for they are all saints of God like you and like me." This is one way: to actually identify these people among us and understand that our job is to love, revere, accept and embrace them as essential parts of our lives. Where is "my" Mary, "my" Joe, "my" newborn on the road?

Another way is to listen to God call you into relationship with these people. Meditations with the Virgin, Joseph and Jesus at hand are valuable ways of experiencing their lives in ways that are meaningful and in ways that can and will change over the years, as you change, as your faith grows, your insight deepens, your love expands, and your compassion and patience rule the day.

For this is what the story is all about: Compassion and patience. God's compassion and patience with us; our compassion and patience with one another, particularly those we are not naturally drawn to. The teen mom, weird old man and accompanying newborn are unbelievably sacred in the spiritual scheme of things. If we don't have room in the houses of our heart for them, at least we should let them hang out in the stable on the property. That is a first step: show them the barn.

We have so much in the houses of our hearts that we do not, in fact, have room for anybody, certainly not this group. But we want to do the right thing, so we show them the barn, and that is good! Who knows? Maybe they'll wait around till a room clears up; after all, they can pay their way—they asked for a room, there just wasn't one available. Or maybe they'll move along according to the old man's voices.

Show them the barn. That is good. If you have room in your heart, go ahead and let them a room. They can pay: Mary, Joe and Jees can pay their bills. You have nothing to worry about there. So how about it? The house? The barn? Whatever you have is better than the side of the road. And who knows? You just might enjoy their company.

Merry Christmas!

Bicycle Meditation

Why Ride a Bike?

- To get you somewhere when you don't have other transportation.

- To get you somewhere before you're old enough to drive.

- To get good exercise and compete in cycling sports events.

- Learning to ride a bike is an important part of growing up.

- It's fun.

- It doesn't pollute the air with fossil fuel fumes.

- A bike is cheaper than a car to buy and maintain.

Why Not to Ride a Bike?

- Not much use in bad weather.

- Takes a long time to get anyplace compared to a car.

- Easy to steal unless you have big locks.

- No room for passengers; everyone has to have a bike.

Why Learn to Listen to God?

• Keeps you connected to God when you have no other means at hand.

• You can live in relationship with God at any age.

• You develop a rapport with God that keeps you spiritually healthy and fit.

• Learning to listen to God is an important part of growing up spiritually.

• It's fun.

• It blesses the earth instead of harming it.

• Listening and building rapport with God is an inexpensive way to be happy.

Why Not Learn to Listen to God?

• Not much use when you want to be nasty and mean.

• God may not respond to you as fast and snappy as you'd like.

• You have to take care of the relationship and protect it.

• You have to have your own relationship, you can't ride with someone else's.

Just something to ponder while you're wheeling through life.

Forgiveness Lesson

Forgiveness is fine, necessary. However, most of the sinning we do (sin being anything we do or say that makes it harder for someone to love God or his/her neighbor or him/herself) arises out of wounds to our heart that are not healed. Continuing, half the reason the wounds are not healed is that they are overrun with parasites that feed on the open sores. These parasites are what scripture calls demons; nasty critters that inhibit healing and call more shots than you'd like to think.

So, if we want to stop a good bit of sinning and having to get forgiven for the same old sin time after time, we have to get rid of the wounds and heal up. This means getting rid of the demons that cause infection.

The principal demons that inhabit our wounds are fear and anger. There are others, of course, hatred, hypocrisy, and so on. How to get rid of them? You present yourself to God for their removal, and you allow the removal. There are large numbers of angels that work in the cleaning and healing field, and they will take care of this work. When you first begin, sometimes it is very intense and you can actually feel the work—the parasites getting pulled out and removed. At first it seems to go on for days. But then it lets up. However, casting out demons is spiritual housecleaning—like dust bunnies they build up completely unawares. Therefore, after the initial big clean, it is good to take time weekly or every couple of weeks to present yourself for this casting out work. You don't have to do the cleaning; you simply have to present yourself.

Once the parasites are gone, the wounds in your heart can start to heal. Again, there is angel work that attends to this, but you have to take the time and allow the work. A few minutes a day is fine, even for the healing of old and deep wounds. Just like your body, very little healing is "instant." Some wounds take constant attention over many years. But, as long as you are engaged in allowing healing, improvement will occur. Like casting out the demons (also called the cleansing of all unrighteousness), healing needs to be addressed regularly for the best progress to be made.

Notice in scripture that Jesus sends out the disciples to cast out demons and heal. He does this way before he goes on about forgiving. Fear and anger and hurt cause so much of the destructive things we say and do to ourselves and others. They cause so much sin, so much repetition of the same sin, so much need for forgiveness. We can begin to break the cycle by allowing our demons to be removed and our wounds to heal, and by allowing these things regularly. By letting God and God's angels clean out the parasites and heal up our wounds, we feel better and we reduce our incidences of sin.

Not a bad arrangement, right? And to think all we have to do is show up. Not bad!

Taking Care
of God

God lives in two places: in you and outside of you. You have two jobs:

One: taking care of the God within you.

Two: having a relationship with the God outside of you.

Tips for your first job:

- The God within needs to be fed and not go hungry.

- The God within needs to be given something to drink and not go thirsty.

- The God within needs to be welcomed and not treated like an outsider, a stranger.

- The God within needs to be clothed and not be naked.

- The God within needs to be nurtured to health and not be sickly.

- The God within needs to be free and not in prison.

Tips for your second job:

- Show up for the relationship.
- Be respectful of that person.
- Listen to the person you are relating to.
- Respond to what you hear.
- Do things together.
- Enjoy each other.
- Mature and rest with each other.

How-to's for your first job:

- Take some time each day to love the God within; this is food.
- Take some time to enjoy the God within; this is water for the soul.
- Take some time to be a friend to the God within; this is hospitality.
- Take some time to share with the God within; this makes God safe.
- Take some time to stimulate the God within; this is nurture.
- Take some time to play with the God within; this is power.

How-to's for your second job:

- Make time for God and God to be together.

- Show respect for both the God within and the God without.

- Don't talk first; listen first.

- Respond to what you hear vs. simply spouting your agenda.

- Take small steps when starting on acts God invites you to do together.

- Rejoice and play cheerfully and often.

- Be comfortable in each other's presence; in down times and in bold ones.

Start-up tip:

Take time daily, but only as much as you know you can take regularly. No starting great guns and quitting. Just a little, each day.

Discipline!

The word with the bad reputation in many circles is the most important word in not just spiritual practice but just about every other. Its association with abusive punishment, imposed torture and other forms of inflicted human damage has legitimacy, for sure. But its association with foundation building, skill strengthening and the development of solid platforms for enormous creativity is every bit as real and legitimate as the negative stuff; even more so. It just doesn't get the same respect. Three reasons for discipline:

Discipline is the skeleton on which God builds the person you are supposed to be. It is your regular return to relationship with God that stabilizes you spiritually and provides the framework within which you are spiritually safe, nurtured and empowered. In short, within which you grow and mature. A disciplined return to relationship means a commitment to listening and responding. While you may not be good at listening and responding at first, with disciplined return to relationship you will become good.

You get good at something by doing it over and over. You may be one of the few people on earth who can go to the Olympic Games having never worked at your sport, you may be one of the few people who can play at Carnegie Hall without prior engagement with your instrument, you may be one of the few people who can radiate spiritual heath and fitness without having developed any spiritual practices. Most of us need to do things over and over to get good at them. We need to do those things regularly and often whether we "feel" like it or not. If you rely on your feelings for practice towards excellence, you're probably not going to make any sustainable progress. Rely on discipline, you'll get there.

Discipline provides the platform for your creativity in your spiritual life as in any other part. While your life may be punctuated by "aha!" moments here and there during which some part of your spirit was planted, rearranged or brought to life, the "aha!" moments are not enough nurture for your spirit to bring you into your wholeness and power. Return to relationship every day, listen to God, respond within the relationship. Not fancy food, but nourishing. The creative and original glow from your regular practice and discipline will feed a hungry heart here, comfort a fearful heart there, forgive a knotted heart some place else, and lighten the burden of suffering that we as human beings cause and carry with us.

Discipline! With it, Peace, Joy and Love have a chance in this world. With it, Justice, Kindness and Humility thrive. With it, Forgiveness, Healing and Cleansing take place. With it, Blessings, Thanksgivings and Praise bring us into the persons we are supposed to be. Discipline! The holy gift, the holy tool, the holy means by which we live with God.

Jesus

If you don't read the Gospels a lot, or if you just go with sound-bite type stories making some solemn Sunday morning point, you miss a lot about Jesus. You miss the guy as a human being, you miss any sense of time, and you miss things kind of hanging together. Some people would say this is okay, because there's not a shred of verifiable historic truth about Jesus in Matthew, Mark, Luke or John. But the Gospels were written to give you the life of a real human being, even one we know spare little about. If you just read (or learn) this story, that parable, this miracle—all as discrete things—Jesus is profoundly unreal. He becomes the wallboard on which you slap post-it notes—a sort of "pin the story on the person" game, with all the flesh-and-blood reality of a paper doll or a Jesusville game.

The first way to insert a little reality into the Jesus "issue" is to nail down a timeline. This timeline is undoubtedly dodgy in parts, but dodgy is better than nothing. Time is important to human beings and it's important to allow Jesus to live in time even if the facts aren't lined up just right. The two time things Jesus shares with all of us—getting born and dying—are fairly well covered, but the in between space is fairly timeless in most of our understandings. For instance, we forget that Jesus went to Egypt after being born in Bethlehem, not back to Nazareth. We lose sight of the fact that at some point he moved to Capernaum from Nazareth and used that town as a base for his operations. We get fuzzy on how much time he actually "worked" his ministry—years? 18 months? 3+ years? It's not so much the exact time that matters as is the fact that he had a fairly short run of it in a public sense. We miss the fact that he was socially pretty well connected as were his disciples—they knew a lot of people all over the place. He was a real, normal guy in many respects. If you only play pin-the-story-on-the-person you miss this.

Another way to keep Jesus a real person is to ride easy with his normal out-of-it behaviors we all share. Time in "the zone"—his mother has to jump start his miracle ministry at Cana: "It's not my time," he tells her. She pays no attention. He gets the wine going. Abusing power when nervous—Jerusalem is going to be dangerous and difficult: act weird and zap the fig tree for not blooming out of season. White lie time: Are you going to Jerusalem? No. Goes. Impatient with bozos: send disciples out on a field trip to cast out demons and heal. Is rested, renewed and enthusiastic on their return "I saw the devil fall from heaven!" There are lots of funny little cameos like these that keep the person real, relatable, and a C+ student of daily living just like the rest of us.

And the best way of all to enfold all this into your system is to read the Gospels every day. They are not the oldest pieces of New Testament writing, but they are the ones that keep Jesus central, not just "about Jesus" central. One chapter a day will do it. Start at Matthew, read through John and go back to Matthew 1 the next day. Over and over. You don't have to pay attention; you just have to do it. Just like with the people you know well: you don't have to pay attention, you just have to show up and be there.

Be Ye Perfect...

...even as your heavenly father is perfect. What a sentence—and not just in terms of language but in terms of judge and/or jury deliberation: We're done for!

What could possibly be meant by such a comment? Of course it is a call to our higher nature, but still we know we are going to fall short time and time again. How can we answer this call to perfection, this command?

There is only one way. And that is to understand perfect not in terms of all our actions but in terms of how we activate the skills and use the tools we are given to live effectively within the great commandment to love God, our neighbors, ourselves.

We are all given the skill to live effectively. We do not know how to activate many of these skills. We are all given the ability to breathe in peace, to be filled with peace. We are all given the ability to drink in joy and we are all given the ability to feed on love and be nourished by it. It is these three intakes, love, joy and peace, that enable our effective actions: because of them we can act with justice, because of them we can be kind, because of them we can walk humbly with our fellow creatures on the face of this earth. When we learn how to use these tremendous skills, we find we live effectively; we approach the perfection God asks of us. Do we get it wrong from time to time? Sure. But that's okay—we are diligent about the skills.

So, too, we can learn to use the tools for effective living. While the skills involve life issues, the tools are those we use to strengthen and repair our ongoing life. The enabling tools are learning to bless and be blessed, learning to thank and be thanked, learning to praise and be praised. The reparative tools are learning to forgive and be forgiven, learning to heal and be healed, learning to cleanse and be cleansed. All of these tools we can use and learn to use effectively. They are gifts we have been given.

Be ye perfect even as your heavenly father is perfect. Be peaceful, just, joyful, kind, loving and humble. Be receptive to these things. Forgive when you need to, be forgiven when you need to, be part of a person's healing, allow yourself to be healed and for healers to be in your life. Help people get clean—free of parasites like anger, fear, hypocrisy, hatred, and the like; and let people help you get clean of the very same things. Allow God and God's angels help in all this too.

Be ye perfect even as your heavenly father is perfect. Use your skills, use your tools. You have skills that can always be refined, tools you can always use. That's the perfection—not "getting it right " but "getting it together" when things need getting: the right skill, the right tool, the right help from God, God's angels, your neighbors and yourself.

Go! Be of good cheer, I have overcome the world—by you using your skills and you using your tools. Thank you!

Peace and Justice

How do you make peace and justice sound like attractive personal goals? You don't. Rather, you try to change people's thinking so that they see, practice, and therefore know that peace and justice are not goals; they are starting points for safe and healthy living. So here we go, changing your thinking.

Peace. Peace is like the air you breathe. If oxygen is essential to the body and its functioning, peace is essential to the spirit and its functioning. You don't have to believe this, but you can practice and experiment with it and see that it is true.

Breathe in peace. You do this by breathing it in with oxygen. Sense that it moves in with the oxygen, drawing down the back of your lungs. Breathe it out and in again. Breathe in and out. Your body and your spirit work together on this. As a discipline, intentionally breathe in peace daily. A good starting place is three breaths in a row, three times a day. Intentionally. Believe it or not, you already do this unintentionally, but intentional will give you a satisfaction you will like. You will come to appreciate and notice the peace you breathe, the airy environment in which your spirit lives.

Justice. If justice is too politicized a word for you, change it to "share." Share with other people. Share until they are safe, or more safe because of your sharing. That is what justice means: sharing so that your neighbor is safe. Intentionally share.

Share who you are and what you have: You can share your toys, your money, your food, your gifts and skills, your tools, your sense of humor, your time. Actually share. Thinking about sharing is like thinking about exercise; it mostly makes you feel guilty. Actually share something you have or are. You already do this unintentionally, but be intentional about it, three times a week to start. Sharing or justice is a baseline discipline for the human race. There are no options for it, just like there are no options for breathing in oxygen and peace. We teach kids to share right off; we need to keep after that kid in us, sharing until it is built into who we are. That is justice; sharing intentionally and regularly.

The point. Peace and doing justice are your foundation stones when it comes to building a safe and healthy life for yourself, your family and others. Lay a firm foundation of peace in your own life and you will inspire others to do the same. You don't have to talk about peace to inspire people, your life will take care of that. People will want the firm foundation you have. Same with justice or sharing. Make just acts part of your foundation and you will find again that people will be inspired to do the same. When we are peaceful, when we share, people know we are safe to be with, and we know we are safe in a spiritually profound way. Change your thinking: start with peace, start by sharing. Be safe because of both. Build a foundation before you develop some goals.

Plan B

Without exception, all of us are living some Plan B in our lives, or maybe a plan even further down the alphabet.

Plan B goes into place when Plan A—our perfect world scenario—does not work. Plan B is a good thing: Plan A doesn't work; try something else. We all know people who spend a hard lifetime either trying to make Plan A work or crying because it didn't work. These people are unhappy, sad, frustrated. Stuck. In some part of most of our lives, we can relate to them; something didn't or doesn't work and we are stuck; we have no Plan B.

Plan B is a good thing. Plan B generally involves a little more humility, a little more listening to God and being with God. Plan B is saying, "Okay, what now?" and listening for what might be the next step. Sometimes it takes us a long time to get to Plan B, but, when we are there, we are happier than we would have ever been with Plan A.

Sometimes we don't have a picture of what Plan B is. This is a God thing: when we switch to Plan B, we listen to God, open up to hear whether we are aware of it or not. God rarely shares "the plan." What God shares is "the next step," and that is probably pretty little. We hear, "How about this?" and it's a little thing. "Why not?" we respond; our grand plan is fallen, why not at least do something. So we do the little thing. Then after a while, another. Gradually Plan B takes shape—in our wake, not in our future.

Plan B is a God plan. We have not generated it, God has, and God walks us into it. Plan B we are not invested in, but God seems to be. We have taken the time to hear, we have taken the time to listen, we have taken the time for God to share both self and others with us. With Plan A we often ask God to assist us in its implementation. With Plan B, God often suggests we walk a step or two with God.

When we live into Plan B, we find we are freer than we ever knew it was possible to be. We don't have to accomplish anything; we simply are obedient to our relationship and to the next step. That doesn't mean Plan B is without suffering, but the suffering is different—it is generally in smaller increments, and because we are walking with God, we are not alone. The burden is lighter. There is time to rest and enjoy life. With Plan B, our self is nurtured. We are less lofty, but we feel better about ourselves. More connected, more humble, more loving, more free.

Plan B—the great resurrection plan after our dreams have died. Plan B—God's plan. Plan B—Plan BE for the human race.

Thanks be to God!

Who Cuts Your Hair?

Remember Samson? The strong guy whose hair was cut off by Delilah and who therefore lost all his strength? The story ends up with a reasonably "happy" ending— with Samson's hair growing back and him pulling down the supports of a temple causing its crash and the death of a whole lot of important enemies (and himself).

You can read all about it in Judges 13-16. There are lots of good themes running through this story. It's an archetypal one, very "myth," like Hercules. Nice for a scriptural wander anytime you are feeling like one.

The point for today is: Who or What Cuts your Hair? Who or what takes away your strength and what goes on so that you get in that kind of a situation where you lose your strength and have to wait for its return? All of us have these areas in our life—physical, mental, spiritual. Some of these areas we have dealt with just fine, and have learned how to protect ourselves, wire around them, deal with them in some way that allows us to be strong and functional no matter what.

But sometimes there are one or two areas where it takes almost nothing—a haircut—and there we are again—down on the floor, blind, confused, hurt and weak, waiting for a restoration we hope will come. We probably know these areas and can lift them to Christ.

It is God's pleasure to lead us and assist us into sustainable, functional strength. God wants us to have long, beautiful hair that we are not tempted to let others cut or chop off ourselves. God wants us to be strong, to have great endurance in the face of this or that, to be flexible enough so that we can deal healthily with both the common and uncommon situations and people we come in contact with. We are to walk blessed through life.

The deal is this, however: God will not impose this health, will not wrestle the scissors out of your or another's hand and throw them away. What God will do is be with you each step, guide your steps, your choices, and "lead you not into temptation and deliver you from evil." Sometimes these steps are so small that you have to learn to walk slower and more tiny than you ever have before. Sometimes there are long waits between steps. All this causes you to be impatient; but you have to remember: for success, God sets the pace, the course, the final destination. Your job is to follow, no matter how slowly.

You make a mistake and let your hair get cut? The good thing about the hair and strength analogy is that the hair always grows back—it is programmed to do so. Your strength will always return—it is programmed to do so. This time, when you are sitting blind, hurt, weak, and hairless, let God take your hand. Let God lead you through whatever slow tasks there are to follow while your hair grows back. Learn to trust. Like Samson, you may never get your sight back, but you will get your hair. You will be strong, your enemies will be overcome, and even if you die and are hated by all, "not a hair of your head will perish."(Luke 21:18) That is God's promise: your strength will endure.

1, 2-2

"What is the greatest commandment?" the guy asked. Jesus replied, "'Love God with all your heart, soul and mind.' That is the first. The second is, 'Love your neighbor as yourself.'"

So how are we doing on this? First: Loving God with ALL our heart, soul and mind? Probably getting about a C-, which is an okay/great grade in Christianity which is a hard religion. And even if we're doing a little less than C-, we still KNOW that loving God is supposed to be number one even if we have other things cluttering up the relationship.

It is good to work intentionally on this a couple of times a year; taking time to do a little spiritual housecleaning and checking what it's like to love God first with ALL your heart, soul and mind. It is good to experience that intentionally.

Now on to loving your neighbor as yourself. Many of us have been raised in the 1, 2, 3 system: God first, neighbor second, yourself third and last. We have worked hard at that. But clearly it's not what the commandment says; the commandment says 1, 2-2— you and your neighbor are to be loved equally.

What is difficult in life, and what Jesus and others we admire are so good at, is balancing neighbor and self equally. Many of us get weighed down in the neighbor arena, doing wondrous good works for others and nothing for ourselves. Others of us fly off the other direction, reaching notable levels of self nurture without much care for fellows around us near or far.

The way you find out where you are is to quote the 2-2 to yourself in a couple of ways: 1) Am I loving my neighbor as much as I love myself? 2) Am I loving myself as much as I love my neighbor? It is pretty easy to catch the imbalance. The next step is doing something about it.

If you are very deficient in self nurture, don't expect to go to the head of the class in this category right away. Just do a little something that gives you direct joy. You're an expert in derivative joy (being happy because you were helpful and made someone else happy); you're not so good at direct pleasure, may not even know what any of it could be. Similarly, if you know how to give yourself a good time and make yourself happy, don't expect to go to the top of the class in outreach ministry right away if ever. Do a little something to experience derivative pleasure—the joy that comes from helping another.

All of us have various levels of experience of both already, but the point is to strive for balance. Naturally there are times when you give all for others, and times when you take every minute for yourself and both are correct. But the idea is to strive for an overall balance between the two—your neighbor and yourself—both of you giving and receiving under the protectorate of God who loves you with all God's heart, soul and mind.

The Guest Book

Here's a way to go about entertaining God: Consider that your heart has a guest book near the door. Guests sign in when the come to visit. You have visiting hours now and then during which you unlock the door so people can come in, sign the book and stay a while.

If you stay conscious during visiting hours, say a while in the morning or some set time in the afternoon or evening, you will not only be able to greet your guests better, you can see that they are comfortable. You will have a nice time with them, as visitors to the heart are wonderful people who are fun, glad and low maintenance. You will enjoy them.

Only allow as much time for visiting hours as you know you can take regularly. Better to have a ten-minute window each day than plan for a big open house once a month, which invariably gets canceled or you get bored, impatient waiting and finally close up early. But the ten-minute window, the guests know about it and will show up right away.

Wonder who they will be? Well you don't have to know ahead of time because they will sign your book. Maybe love will come by a bit, or peace or joy or a happy spirit from long ago. Maybe biblical or saintly types from your life will come by. Who knows? Just look at the book if you can't tell right away and you will know. The visitors always identify themselves.

After your heart has entertained a bit and gotten the hang of it, maybe you can suggest a little stroll with a friend or two through the neighborhood. You and your companion can look at life together—people walking, animals, trees and grass, weather of all kinds. Maybe one of your friends will invite you take a trip with them. Probably just a little one like the ones you've been taking.

No set-up needed for this hospitality project. You have a guest book in your heart whether you've been using it or not. It's right by the door. Open it, open the door to your heart, and see who comes in. It won't take long before you and your friends are loving this time together.

Scared of Listening?

A whole lot of people are scared of listening to God. What if God said to move to Africa or sell everything and give to the poor? God has all sorts of traumatic opportunities to choose from! Better to keep the head down, stay quiet, say nice prayers, do thoughtful things, go to church, and be helpful off and on.

What is scary about listening to God is that you have no idea what God is going to say. This is true. But it's still worth the listen, because time after time God says something comforting. "I am here," or something like that. "I love you." God is rarely chatty and always supportive, of YOU; maybe not your plans, but YOU.

The fact is you can't have a relationship with someone if you never listen to them. You may think you can have one, but you can't. We all say we want a relationship with God, but then we act like we don't want one. We bark orders at God through our prayers, give God suggestions on how to run the universe (at least our part of it), but rarely accord God the same privilege in return. That's probably why we're afraid; we're afraid God will bark orders at us and give us suggestions we don't want to take.

One bit of good news is that God is nicer than we are. More patient, kind, generous and understanding. Another bit of good news is that God is always present to listen to us AND answer us. When we don't hear anything, here are some things that may have happened:

1. You gave God a nanosecond to respond. God didn't barge in, take control of the conversation, wrestle you to the ground and force you to listen, so you heard nothing.

2. You listened for only what you wanted to hear. You said something, God said nothing back, enough already.

3. You did not let God start the conversation.

4. You selected a station in your heart through which God was allowed to broadcast but have not opened the bandwidth to see if reception is better elsewhere.

Because of the unknown factor, you may always be a little bit afraid when you take the time to listen to God. But if you will let God start the conversation, you will never be disappointed. Show up. Let God open your heart if you're afraid to. Listen. First it just may be silence and God's presence you "hear." Later it may be just a word or two. It will never be anything that hurts, it will be something that fulfills and warms the heart.

On the rare times there are "directions" you hear, they will be matter of fact to you. "Move to Africa" will be as matter-of-fact as "take a rest." Why? Because of who you are and who you have become as a result of your relationship with God: listening, responding, listening again.

Brains and God

Is God smart? Smarter than any one of us? Does God think things over, come to a decision, then, well, then what? Has God got any brains at all? If God is some kind of a "divine mind" how does that mind function? Is God a big ball of energy physicists like to explore and poke around in? Is God "God" at all? Is God some useful human construct and coping mechanism? Makes you tired to think about all of it.

God is best known through experience. When it comes to knowing God, the receptor for experience is located in your body, not your head. Your head can analyze the experience, play with it, poke around with it, but it can't be the initial receptor of the God experience. It is your nervous system, particularly its receptors in your heart area and spine that responds to the presence and reality of God. Your head is handmaid to your heart; heart first, head next, along with other receptors.

The people who seem smartest about God are those who operate on this understanding. To try to make your head/brains go first in knowing God is to use a secondary receptor, one that can contribute to the whole but isn't the first line of understanding.

A parallel: your mouth is the principal receptor for food that nourishes your body. You can stuff food in your ear or your eyes and nose, but why when you have such a satisfactory first line receptor? Your eyes, ears and nose can contribute to your understanding and enjoyment of food, but they are not the primary receptors of this nourishment. So again, your nervous system receptors in your upper torso and your spine are your primary spiritual receptors to which your mind, eyes, nose, ears, fingers, etc. can contribute, but they do not come first.

Back to brains and God: Is God smart? Answer: Sure. God seems to have good survival skills that aren't dependent on really anything, and that is a measure of smarts that the planet at least seems to admire. Believe in God, don't believe, have a relationship, ignore—God seems to motor along pretty evenly through any of the above.

What is important, though, are brains and us. Are we smart when it comes to our relationship with God? Are we sensible about letting our heart and soul experience God and then letting our brain work with that if it wishes to? Are we up for knowing God the way God is best known, heart open and listening for God's presence? Or are we more comfortable stuffing food in our ear, God thoughts in our brain, and leaving our primary receptors unused?

We want to use the primary receptors. We may have been poorly taught about spiritual health and awareness of God, but we can unlearn all that in a jiffy; because our receptors are ready and waiting to be used; and God is right there to say Hi and fill our hearts with gladness.

Feasts and Faith

You can lay on a feast but you can't lay on faith. Faith has to be grown. Like a well tended crop of any sort, well tended faith is beautiful and strong, healthy and fit.

Sunday is a feast day. You can attend a great feast every week with a fine selection of sacraments, prayers, music, preaching and the rest. You can enjoy this celebration and be fed by it. You can maybe take in so much you don't have to be nourished spiritually for any number of days. But eventually the effects of feasting wear off. "How soon is it till Sunday?" your spirit asks. "When can I take in nourishment again?"

Sunday-fed faithfulness—only Sunday—doesn't really have a chance to grow well and mature. True, there are a few spirits for whom it is just fine; but for most of us, a little more frequent tending is in order. We need to be watered more than once a week, we need some good clean air to breathe, we need our soil turned over and enriched to stimulate our roots and shoots.

We need daily bread, water and air more than a banquet if the truth be told. Living from banquet to banquet is exhausting for the soul. Regular daily nourishment is more relaxing, easier on the system, and healthier in the long run.

Daily food for the soul is always available. There is always peace to breathe and be enfolded in. There is joy to drink in each day, to bathe in and rejoice in. There is love of all sorts all around to feed on—the love of other people, the food of music, art, nature—God in a million ways. This is always available; it is the nourishment God provides for each one of us, every day.

We do need to take time to take it in. Regular meals are good. Sitting in God's presence three times a day and allowing ourselves to be fed peace, joy and love is a very good thing to do. Sometimes the offerings are simple, in fact most of the times they are—a simple joy, a simple experience of peace, a simple slice of love of one sort or another. But they are real and they are food. You take them in through your heart and through your spinal chord.

If you eat regularly, your spirit is increasingly healthy and increasingly secure. It does not have to worry about eating just once a week. It knows it is fed every day and that it can always rely on that nourishment to be present. It can go to the feast on Sunday and enjoy the offerings without having to worry about trying to take in enough to last a week. It can be happy and it can grow up.

Mature faithfulness is a beautiful plant. Beautifully nourished itself, it provides nourishment for others. It is healthy, strong, reliable and sure. It is each one of us when we take the time to be taken care of.

Casting Out Demons

The slightly weird language may make you uneasy, but what it points to is absolutely essential for your spiritual life. One of the biggest spiritual problems today is the fact that folks have "cast out" the understanding and practice of casting out demons along with the uncomfortable language.

Casting out demons, or its equivalent term, "cleansing of all unrighteousness," refers to getting rid of things like anger, fear, hatred, hypocrisy and the like. These are the parasites that feed on our wounds and inhibit their healing as long as they are around. Their presence is one of the reasons that healing often takes longer than it should: we don't get the wounds cleaned so that they can heal fresh and uninfected.

If you'll notice Jesus, his first assignment for the disciples is to get out the good news and cast out demons. Healing and forgiveness come later. The disciples' job is first, to talk up how easy it is to be healthy, whole and have a great relationship with God; and second, to help people learn about getting rid of the critters than infect most wounds thus hold up health.

Casting out demons is not difficult. All you do is ask for it: "Get rid of the demons," or "Cleanse me," does it. You can repeat these. You will have a sense of things being lifted out and/or washed away. You allow this to happen. You can do it in a crisis, or you can clean up regularly, like before you go to bed or when you get up.

Who does the work? Angels, God, Jesus—whoever is sent. Doesn't matter. Cleansing is one of the easiest things to happen. You feel fresh. Your wounds are still there—broad lacerations, deep punctures or whatever, but now the healing hands of God and God's can work to ease your pains and make you well.

When the infections are gone and the healing takes place, your life improves. You feel better, you sin less. How so? Most of our sinning—saying and doing things that make it more difficult for people to love God, their neighbors or themselves—comes from our deep and infected wounds: we strike out to protect the horrible, enormous and unhealed hurts we carry around within us.

Give it a try. Ask for cleansing. Allow the washing. Allow the healing afterward even if it takes time. The healing teams of heaven are there and prepped for work. Think of it—washing away hate, anxiety, fear, anger, the rest. Clean wounds with a chance to heal; a whole life in the offing. Sounds like a deal.

Worth a try.

Rest

The creation story in the Bible has God resting on the last day. Was God tired? Maybe. A whole lot of stuff had been created. But this is instructive: If the universe/God needs rest after a major spurt of creation, the chances are that we do, too. Creation involves chaos—you throw a lot of stuff out there into the unknown. If you believe in yourself and follow your irrepressible urge to create, you throw it out there and hope with joy. You know that the divine sparks you send out will result in creation of some sort, plus the inevitable creation byproducts— dust, used up stuff, mess, etc.

So lesson one: We should rest after we create.

The creation story also has God enjoying God's creation. When you are busy creating, you don't take time to enjoy anything other than the act of creating. Enjoying what you have created comes later—at the end of the day, the week, the lifetime. When you create you don't look backward or forward, you look "right now," intent upon what you are doing. Only afterward, in that rest spot, and when the edge is off the exhaustion, is there sitting back and looking at what took place. We are pleased, in accordance with the truth of our creation; it is a real expression of our soul. It may not "work" or it may. It may be an inspiration for yet another creation or steadfast on its own. It may relate to values and cultures in place or it may point another way. It is our truth for that day and we can enjoy it, satisfied.

So lesson two: we should take time to enjoy our creation within our rest.

The creation story doesn't cover every kind of rest, but it covers a kind of rest that is important for our completeness as human beings. We create, we rest, we enjoy our creation within that rest. Sometimes we forget about the imperative to create and rest. Yet looking at our lives, those are the times we remember and appreciate best: the times we created and, resting afterwards, enjoyed all that we had made. If you feel the irrepressible urge to create has gone to sleep somewhere along the way, take a rest, a creation rest. The imperative will wake up fast. Let it charge, then go forth to create and rest again. What was God doing before all that creation work? Chances are God was having a rest.

So lesson three: we should rest in order to create again and keep creating always.

Spiritual Sloth

There is such a thing as a Spiritual Couch Potato, someone who is content to click through religious stuff from the pew, the recliner, the couch, the bed. All of us do this from time to time, but it's not such a good idea to do it all the time, not very healthy, not very whole.

Some of this sloth and spiritual inactivity comes from over reliance, consciously or not, on the forgiveness message: no matter what you do or don't do, no matter how many times you drop the ball or flat out don't play, you are forgiven and right with God. The fact is, that is true.

But another fact is, by watching faith stuff only—whether at church, or on TV, or in books—and never really getting with the program, you don't develop your spiritual dimension at all. You don't get spiritually healthy and fit. It's like watching sports and reading exercise books—it doesn't do much for your personal heath and fitness, though you may be up to date on statistics and information.

Let's think about that Bible story of the three servants entrusted with money while the master is out of town doing something or other. One is given ten coins and makes ten more—energetic guy; one is given five coins and makes five more—again a go-getter; one is given one coin and stashes it away—a financial Couch Potato who has rationalized the pros of staying with the status quo. We all know that the two investors reap great rewards both financially and in praise, and that the do-nothing man gets nothing but a seriously severe dressing down from the boss. He reaps no reward for himself, he gets no praise.

Feature yourself as one of the three servants entrusted with a gift from the boss. The gift this time is a beautiful spirit, not a coin. You can invest it, and invest in it—by developing and maintaining disciplines that increase its health and fitness, or you can Couch Potato it and let it just sit around undeveloped. The choice is yours.

To make your choice, keep this in mind: You would not have been entrusted with this beautiful spirit if you did not also come with the wherewithal and skill to make it grow, bloom, flourish, and be like Christ among us. You don't have to do it, and you will be forgiven if you don't. But you can do it if you wish, and by doing so come to know a fullness of life that simply can't show up if all you do is sit there on the pew, the couch, the chair or the bed.

Potato or prophet, lump or lunatic: Which shall it be? Let me give you a tip before you choose: in the faith world, the lunatics always win!

God's Answer to your St. Francis Prayer

I have made you an instrument of my peace.
   THEREFORE

Where there is hatred, you must sow love.
Where there is injury, you must pardon.
Where there is discord, you must unite.
Where there is doubt, you must provide faith.
Where there is despair, you must bring hope.
Where there is darkness, you must be light.
Where there is sadness, you must provide joy.

You must console those who need consoling.
You must understand those who are misunderstood.
You must love the unloved.

You will receive as you give.
You will be pardoned as you pardon.
You will live forever as you die.

Amen.

And God continues with this assurance:

I am with you as you dedicate your life to peace.
  THEREFORE

I help you love.
I help you pardon.
I help you unite people.
I strengthen your faith.
I embolden your hope.
I fill you with light.
I fill you with joy.

I am your partner in consoling others.
I am your partner in understanding the
  misunderstood.
I am your partner in loving the unloved.

Together we receive and give each other to the
  world.
Together we pardon others and are pardoned by
  them.
Together we'll die, together we live eternally.

Amen.

Show Up

Christianity is a hard religion—at least it is if you are going to live it the way Jesus suggests. It's hard because it is a religion of relationship: you are not obedient to BIG GOD; you are obedient to your RELATIONSHIP with God. You don't spend your life doing what you are told to do by the Ruler of Heaven and Earth; you spend your life living in close, immediate relationship with another human being who is also God.

In many ways we prefer the "do-what-God-says" religion. We like the notion that God has laid down a set of rules and we're supposed to follow them. We get forgiven if we don't. Nice deal. We're pretty good people, we think; so we do our best, mess up here and there, say we're sorry and presto, the balance sheet once again shows a profit. We're in, we're good; heaven awaits.

All of that is true. There's nothing wrong with the do-right religion; it's a good one, it can even feature Jesus as a good guy, and it can assure you a place in the hereafter. But the do-right religion is not exactly the religion that Jesus and the apostles are promoting in the New Testament. They're talking something much more ambitious; they're talking about a relationship, a relationship that can bring you into the fullness of being the way nothing else in the whole world can. They are promoting a relationship that can fill you with joy, and render you powerful, peaceful and kind beyond your wildest dreams.

Your part in this relationship that enables you to be whole and grand is to show up for it. You can't have a relationship with anyone without showing up. That is the baseline for all relationships. And you really have to show up. You can't read about showing up, you can't pretend to show up, you show up. You open up the way you do when you show up at a party, or a neighbor's house, or the first day of school. You don't have to be way open; you can be a little guarded. But you have to show up and you have to be available for relationship if only a little bit.

Christianity is a hard religion, but only because it is different; it is a religion of relationship with another person, Jesus. Beyond adjusting from do-right to show-up, it's pretty easy. Jesus is very interested in showing up for the relationship and building it into something strong, flexible and enduring—for both of you. Because Jesus is a real person, just like you, you will find that the relationship often differs from day to day. You're in a bad mood; he's present but unengaged, etc. etc. It has all the hallmarks of any relationship. That's part of the fun of it, and part of the reason you show up every day or at least regularly—who knows what things will be like today.

In Christianity, God has given us a wonderful opportunity. Human beings grow and thrive in healthy relationships. By giving us an opportunity to live in relationship with Jesus, God has given us the opportunity to thrive beyond any expectation. Jesus is human and incredibly healthy. You live with him, you are the same.

Hand One and Hand Two

Remember this Jesus quote?

If any of you put a stumbling block before one of these little ones who believe in me, it would be better for you if a great millstone were fastened around your neck and you were drowned in the depth of the sea. Woe to the world because of stumbling blocks! Occasions for stumbling are bound to come, but woe to the one by whom the stumbling block comes! (Luke 18:6-7)

Well guess what? The stumbling block business is just about the biggest in the world if not THE biggest. Stumbling block production and distribution are in full swing all over the globe, and right in your hometown, too. Stumbling blocks are those big Stops that prevent you or your neighbor from living the Enough life—enough food, enough water, enough shelter and clothing, enough education, healthcare and employment opportunity, enough for a holiday now and then or a little splurge here and there.

Stumbling blocks are not good. Yet we put up with them. We are more comfortable helping the victims of stumbling block injuries than taking a stand against stumbling block production and distribution. Why? Because stumbling-block makers and distributors are often the people paying the bills. People rich in cash, rich in influence and authority are often sponsors of those who look after stumbling block victims.

This works for them: pay to have folks bandage up the wounded, help the lame walk, the blind see and the good news of health preached to all. This outlay doesn't affect stumbling block producers and distributors at all. And in the USA they can even write off this expenditure from their income taxes. So what if they create barriers to health and the Enough life? They can throw some cash at a hospital or good-work ministry or two and still keep producing and distributing stumbling blocks like mad.

What should people do who think that the stumbling block business should either go out of business or claim cottage industry status at best? They need to do this: to use both the hands that God has given them, not just one. With Hand One, keep on helping the victims stand on their feet, get well, and walk into a safe and health-filled life. With Hand Two, signal STOP! to stumbling-block makers and producers and take real measures to shut them down; real acts—no whiney wistful thoughts or wimpy wishes for someone else to do it. Little acts work; little measures add up.

Learn to use Hand Two. God will teach you. Listen for instructions. When you listen to God, you become unafraid of using Hand Two and saying STOP! to stumbling-block makers and distributors. You become unafraid of possibly losing funding. You become a human being, saying NO to stumbling blocks and YES to the Enough life for everyone. Using Hand Yes and Hand No, you become Christ among us, helping the needy, halting the abusers, fashioning the kingdom of God on earth, the kingdom of Enough.

The Jesus Curriculum

What if we folks were taught the content Jesus taught his disciples at the beginning?

He began with three subjects in his curriculum: the good news, casting out demons, healing. He taught these to the disciples, and afterwards he sent them out on a field trip to practice.

The Good News: This course teaches you to have a healthy and rewarding relationship with God.

Casting out Demons: This course teaches you how to get rid of nasty spiritual parasites (anger, fear, etc.) that infest wounded hearts.

Healing: This course teaches you how to cure wounded hearts so that your relationship with God is healthy and flourishes.

These are required courses, not electives.

We don't hear the disciples whining about how these courses are too hard, or how they can't do them or how they're no good at healing or casting out demons or anything else. They are all happy to learn, happy to practice, happy to report on both their successes and failures, happy to go out and try again. And to think: None of them had taken pre-good news, pre-casting out demons, pre-healing before they signed on to the curriculum! No experience necessary!

Check the curriculum of your local Jesus School to see if these courses are offered, and sign up for them if they are. If they aren't, make it clear to the minister in charge of education just how much you want to take these classes: You want to be a great disciple, and it looks like getting good at these three things is pretty important. No experience necessary! Keep realizing that!

All three classes are rich with things to learn about how to BE in relationship with God. All Jesus classes have a work-study component, so practicing what you learn comes within the same framework as the learning itself. In Christian practice and in these three classes absolutely, the most important thing you will learn is how to be with God. Being with God is the baseline of all the classes, the place you never step out of.

Learning "about" God is not the same as being with God. Learning about God is like learning about food—it isn't the same as eating it. Learning about God may be interesting and insightful, but it won't feed your soul with the nutrients it needs to live to the glory of God and the great good cheer of your fellow human beings. Sign up for the Jesus curriculum, get going on discipleship, enjoy the powerful and illuminating life of Christ.

The Kingdom of Enough

The Kingdom of God on Earth can also be called the Kingdom of Enough. It is not a planet-specific replica of the bejeweled city in Heaven which is paved, walled and built with nothing but the most luxurious, rarest and beautiful the planet has to offer.

The Kingdom of God on Earth is the Kingdom of Enough. It is a place where everybody has enough food, drink, clothing, housing, employment, education and fun. It is a place where everybody is free and safe, supported and nurtured, deeply rooted and comfortable with themselves. It is a Kingdom of Enough; a happy, sustainable place.

To live well in the Kingdom of Enough, and to get there, you have to develop a sense of Enough for yourself. What is Enough? Enough food? Employment? Clothing? Friends? Some people are handy with this knowledge, and some people haven't a clue.

How to develop a clue about Enough? To do this you have to deal with More. There is the sin of More and there is the blessing of More. You are sinning about More when you are compelled to own, eat, have, horde, etc. More than Enough for yourself. You are reaching for a blessing of More when you ask for more clothes when you are naked and cold, more food and drink when you are hungry and thirsty, more work when your job won't cover costs for your family and yourself, more care when you are sick and so on.

Many of us use More to cover up our great anxieties about one thing or another. If we have More money beyond what we need to safely and kindly meet the needs of ourselves and our families, we believe we will feel less anxious. If we have more clothes than we need, we believe that at least we will always have something to wear. If we own More of this, that and anything, we believe that maybe we will be protected from demons, danger and all forms of insecurity. More is our colossal safety blanket.

The bad news—the demons live inside, infecting the wounds that cause the dangers, the insecurities and anxieties. There are a couple of ways to have them leave the nest of the wounds and disappear so the wounds can heal and you can sharpen your sense of Enough. You can ask God to let the angels work on their removal, scraping them off and out of your heart. You can carry some of the hatreds and fears (demons) to the curb yourself where heavenly garbage crews will collect them. You can say thank you.

You can deal with the Sin of More, with the presence of More in your life. More is not bad or evil, nor is it Grand and Righteous. More is More, and it is addressed and lived with correctly or wrongly. To live with More wrongly is sin—to take More than Enough. You can catch yourself and stop and gradually get it right, learn what is Enough and no More for you. You can live with More rightly, take Enough for you and yours, and share the More than Enough with those who need it. You can live in the Kingdom of Enough; the Kingdom of God on Earth. You will love it, and so will everyone.

Nice

You'll be interested to know that Young's Bible Concordance, which lists all the words used in the Bible and the books, chapters and verses where they can be found, has no entry for "nice." Yet "nice" is the word we in the USA use with such careless abandon that "nice" stands for absolutely everything somewhat-to-greatly positive to "not nice," which stands for absolutely everything somewhat-to-greatly negative.

This linguistically lazy way of sizing up things has an extremely negative spiritual effect. Because "nice/not nice" is used so excessively from childhood on up, we have become terrified of being "not nice." "Nice" has become an archetypal human value for us in the USA. To risk being "not nice" is to threaten what we have developed as our baseline guide for human behavior. We are afraid to say something "not nice." We are afraid to act in a way someone would consider "not nice." When someone accuses us of doing or saying something "not nice," we are afraid, worried and guilty. We think how to avoid being "not nice" the next time or how to make up for being "not nice" when we were.

Spiritually, "nice/not nice" is tremendously inhibiting. Its exalted place in the USA value system puts the great values like honesty, truth, right-thinking and clarity in significant and chronic jeopardy. Their place in our value system is secondary at best: it is better to be nice than honest, it is better to be nice than angry at wrongdoing, better to be nice than to stand up against injustice. "Nice/not nice" dulls our sense of justice, peace, joy, kindness, love and humility." We'd rather be nice than accountable to any other value. And, if we stand up against injustice, etc. we'd better be "nice" when we do it!

You can't grow up spiritually and be nice all the time. That is the sad and sorry truth of it all. Turning over the tables of the money changers is not nice; telling Satan to get out of the way when Peter is trying to give Jesus a compliment is not nice. Tons of stuff is not nice. We are dulled and dying because of our irresponsible language that we induct into our smallest people from the get go: "Joey, is it 'nice' to hit Sara?"

What we need to do to be truly honest and accountable human beings is to say "NO!" to our lousy, sloppy language once and for all. We need to search for and use the honorable words of human behavior: "Joey is it 'kind' to hit Sara?" has so much more truth to it than "nice." Nice shades the truth, hides it; being thoughtful about language makes the truth shine. "Nice" has made us morally dull and deeply cowardly as we face the world.

Jesus never talked about nice; nor did Moses, St. Paul, Isaiah, Elijah, the gospel writers, the apostles, the prophets, sinners or saints. Nice needs a holy burial in our lives. Have a good cry, bury it in the ground and turn around. It will take time to learn life without your best four letter friend, but you can do it; and you'll find yourself fresher, stronger and more spiritually healthy because of it.

Spiritual Tune-up

Just the way you can have a "physical exam" you can have a "spiritual exam" if you want one. Lots of people don't know that. Who do you go to for a spiritual exam and/or tune up? You go to people who work in the field of spiritual health and fitness. In a lot of Jewish and Christian stuff these people are called Spiritual Directors. But there are gurus and God-people everywhere whose field is spiritual health, and who can help point you to where it would help if you tightened a spiritual screw or two, cleaned this or that, etc.

Touching base with a spiritual director/spiritual health person is often a good idea. Of course, you can "do it all by yourself" just the way you can "do it yourself" your physical health, but you don't have to. For referrals you can talk to people you know who seem to be spiritually healthy—whatever that means to you. They may know someone. If you belong to a public worship community, someone in that group may know what direction to point you in.

To work a little with your spirit, here are a few questions you can consider:

Is your spirit EMPOWERED? A person with a healthy, powerful spirit is one that is well loved, happy and humble—which means being comfortable with who you are. You can cheer with a group, you can take stands all by yourself and stick with them, your ego doesn't mess you up. You are YOU, fresh and alive even though occasionally tired and discouraged.

Does your spirit get adequate NURTURE? Is there joy going on in a regular way? Does it wash over you and through you? Do you take the time to let this happen? Does kindness come into your life in different ways: Are people kind? Are you kind to yourself? Do the joy and kindness in your life make you healthy and strong?

Are you SAFE spiritually? Is the center of your life peaceful? Do you touch base with this peaceful center regularly? Is your life just? Do you have the rights you need for a healthy life? Do you help secure these rights for yourself and your neighbors when they are withheld or missing and life is therefore unsafe? Do you run away from the world trying to be safe or work within it?

If considering these questions indicates you'd be helped by some "help," you might think about a spiritual consultation or tune up with someone in the business. There are always a few folks who are spiritually healthy from the get-go and never get unhealthy or mixed up. The rest of us, though, can generally use a pointer or two here and there. As with physical health, you don't have to be at death's door spiritually to check out your health. It's a good thing to do when you're healthy, too; or would like to be.

God's okay with you however you are, know that. Just know God's got folks out there to help you if you want them to.

Epiphany, Part Two

The Flight into Egypt. Everybody's got Part One down: The Three Kings. We're less solid on Part Two, but it's every bit as important as Part One, maybe more so.

We all love Part One. Glamorous, exotic, and fun, Part One is made for the imagination, illustrators and Christmas pageants. And the Star is still around, cosmic glamour in the sky. The mainstream "theology" of the visit is happily comfortable—important people from afar coming to worship baby Jesus and bring him presents fit for a king.

Part Two: We get this kind of wrong from the beginning. Unconsciously, our eyes have become unhooked from the baby and his family. We follow the story of the kings—their visit, their decision not to return to tell Herod about it, their departure to places unknown. We then shift our focus not back to the family but onto Herod. The paranoid ruler makes a horrific decision to kill everybody in Bethlehem less than two years old. This ghastly massacre ends our interest in Epiphany, except for the footnote that Joseph heard about what was going to happen, heard God say "Leave and go to Egypt," and did that.

Let's see what happens if we focus on Joseph, Mary and Jesus instead of Herod. Joseph, working and living in Nazareth, has made a quick trip to Bethlehem, his birth village, for a mandated census check. His wife gives birth before they can return. There's lots of commotion in the birth stable but it's all okay. No problems keeping baby Jesus safe and cared for. Then Joseph has a dream:

there's danger for your kid on the prowl; get out of here and go to Egypt. So the three of them leave and stay in Egypt till Herod dies.

Here is where we hit the important part of Epiphany Two: The most important thing in the world is to keep Jesus safe and alive. What started out as a trip from home lasting less than a week has turned into a detour lasting several years. There is no way on God's earth that this could have been anticipated; and certainly it wasn't planned for. But you do what you have to do to keep Jesus safe and alive and flourishing. If you lose your family, friends and work to keep Jesus safe, you lose your family, friends and work.

For us, Epiphany Two means that, like Joseph, we must do whatever it takes to keep the Christ inside of us safe, alive and flourishing. We may be able to continue in place with nothing dangerous to contend with in terms of baby care, but we may have to change our plans, friends, work and expectations, at least some. Keeping Jesus alive within our hearts is what is most important. This is what we learn from Epiphany Two: whatever it takes, small or large, that is our responsibility: keeping the Christ alive within us.

Joseph, Mary and Jesus went to Egypt to be safe. A 250-300 mile journey replaces an 80 mile return trip to Nazareth. As we renew our commitment to the life of Christ within us, let us remember to keep that life safe. We may have to change a few things, make a few detours. But being allowed to keep Jesus within us safe is a privilege, worth every detour, every change of plans, every joy and hardship encountered on the road.

Spiritual Boot Camp

Up for it? Then here's the first thing—if you want to tighten up your spirituality and have some effect on the world: DISCIPLINE

Discipline is good for you. In everything—your spirituality is no exception. You have a spiritual dimension, the way you have a physical dimension, but chances are you are either pretty disciplined about taking care of your body, OR know what you should be doing to take care of your body in order to be healthy.

Spiritual discipline requires you to pay attention to your spirituality every day. It requires you to set up a lifestyle where that attention takes place every day. More than once. Spiritual health requires work. For some people this work is easier than it is for others, for some harder—just like anything else. Hard doesn't mean you don't do it; and if you do it enough and regularly, it becomes less hard—just like anything else.

So, what first: **TAKE SOME INVENTORY** on what you have in place that you call spiritual discipline. Do you go to church regularly, every Sunday? Do you read the Bible every day? Do you belong to a regularly meeting spiritually oriented study group? Do you read 'spiritual' books? Do you say prayers at home?

Next: **SET SOME DISCIPLINE GOALS**. These should not be a simple intensification of what is in place, but some new things. AND, these new goals should be low on "about" stuff and high on "do it" stuff. This means not-much-to-no reading "about" God, the church, St. Paul, or commentaries. That's like reading exercise books: Interesting, but they don't do much for your strength, endurance and flexibility.

FOCUS ON EXPERIENCE, things that require some action or non-action on your part: sitting still for five minutes each day, saying some praises and thanks to God for three minutes each day instead of just petitions, saying a prayer or two outside and out loud with no one around to hear. If you are dependent on a church prayer book or something, set up a weaning program so that you can go alone without a book.

BE STRICT WITH YOURSELF. There is an ocean of flabby spirituality out there. We're drowning in 'potential.' Get up, shape up. Three times a day return to your relationship with God is good. The Muslims have five returns. That's better. Keeps you on a shorter leash. Don't make excuses to yourself. If you have set your goals too high, the way you do with diets, modify them. The rule of thumb is: DON'T DO MORE THAN YOU CAN DO REGULARLY.

The people you recognize for their spirituality are highly disciplined about their spirituality. Discipline inspires trust. And the trust it inspires is this: that you, too, can have a relationship with God that refreshes life. Enlist anytime.

Sin and Forgiveness

Sin is sort of a passé term except maybe for Sunday in church. One of the troubles with this is that it makes forgiveness kind of fuzzy too: if you can't identify sin, it's hard to identify what you need to ask forgiveness for. We sort of mush around thinking that well, what needs to be forgiven are things we feel bad about.

That's okay, but your spiritual life will improve dramatically if you can get specific about sin: what exactly have you done or said that needs to be forgiven. Note: do not confuse your sins (things you have done or said) with the effect of your sins—the hurts they caused, making it harder for someone to love God, or his/her neighbor or him/herself.

You don't get forgiven for hurting someone; you get forgiven for what you said or did that hurt someone. This doesn't feel like enough, because we are sorry and feel guilty about the hurt. But hurts need to heal (generally without you, unfortunately); sins need to be forgiven.

You can learn about sin from the hurt you caused, though. What did you do or say that made someone hurt and wounded their ability to love and be loved? Was it a rude remark; was it a racist act, conscious or unconscious? Was it a presumptuous act? Was it the breaking of a confidence? Sins are very specific. A sinner is a person who sins specifically, AND ONE WHOSE SPECIFIC SINS CAN BE FORGIVEN.

Ask a person to forgive you for a specific sin: Please forgive me for telling Joe the confidence you asked me not to share. That person may forgive you or may not; you have done your part in asking. You ask God the same thing. In fact you can practice with God: "God, please forgive me for telling Joe the confidence Molly asked me to not share."

Accept forgiveness. From God, from individuals and groups when it is offered. Again specifically: "I accept your forgiveness of me for breaking your confidence. Thank you for forgiving me." Forgiveness on a basic level is a contract: "Please forgive me," is a request for no revenge. "I forgive you," means no revenge will be taken.

What about all that hurt? All the ravages sinful words and acts have caused? Those wounds need to be healed. Healing is a different process from forgiveness. We have to take time to heal. Healing is slow. We have to have a healing team, which generally does not include the person whose sin caused the wound. We have to take time for God and the angels to work on the wounds, clean them and hold them in the healing love of Christ.

To be healthy spiritually you have to forgive and be forgiven. You have to allow healing and realize that the process is different from forgiveness. Get specific on those sins and on your requests for forgiveness. Enjoy the release from sin. Enjoy your new health.

Self Respect

This is sort of a hard one. What is self respect built on? How can you respect yourself and put up with all the things you do wrong?

For some people self respect comes easily. These are the lucky ones. For lots of people, self respect is a fragile structure, built on air and constructed with external markers. Have I been a good parent? Spouse? Partner? Friend? Have I done enough for the world, to make it a better place? Have I used all my gifts correctly and effectively, have I effectively lived into the person I was created to be?

For some reason, the "No" response to all these questions comes easily. We are quick to see our shortfalls. Even when we can point to our "successes" they seem irrelevant, and never carry the weight and import of those things we have done wrong, inadequately, or not at all.

We can listen to wise people, our friends, and others who admire us and/or things we do, but these voices have no staying power; they are no match for the negative self evaluation whispering inside. God loves us. Great. So what? God loves everybody.

The God thing is useful, though: If we listen to God and experience God's love of us, we have some rest, some comfort. We aren't all that bad, maybe, if God enjoys us so. And we have a place to go to be safe, safe even from our own relentless negativity. Living off God's love of us is not enough, however. It is a legitimate source of well being, but it is only part of the respect available to human beings; the respect of ourselves is necessary, and actually allows us to accept the respect of God and others more fully.

The ground of Self Respect is wonder. Wonder at life. Wonder at a nice day, wonder at anything. Wonder pulls you back into who you are and keeps you from straining so hard. Wonder sinks roots in the good earth of joy and allows you to look up and spread high if you want to. Wonder keeps you entirely within yourself and yet gloriously a part of this world. Wonder allows you to respect yourself, with laughter even.

When you wonder you are confidently, absolutely you. Wonder allows you to respect your character, for better and for worse, and to have a solid respect for all that you have accomplished. Wonder allows you to accept the gracious respect of others. Wonder allows you to be forgiven for real sins and dismissive of the imaginary ones you used to bolster your self loathing. Wonder allows you to heal and gives you the patience to heal.

Wonder is the ground of who you are, the roots of who you are. Wonder allows you to say to God, "Yes, you are right, I am wonderfully made." Every time you start to outrun your wonder, pull back. Every time you are oppressed by failure, stop: let wonder resurge and be your roots again. You are wonderfully made. Rejoice and be glad in it.

The Snake—
Still Winning!

That serpent in the Garden of Eden is the most successful of God's creatures. He may be living on his belly, but he's sly and crafty and still tricking us every time. We have learned nothing; every time he suggests we do a little something that won't really harm us, we say okay. We bite. We suffer the consequences.

The snake is that little sliver in our consciousness that says, "It doesn't really matter," even though God says it does. The snake allows us, encourages us even, to see opportunity and permission as one and the same: If we can do it, we should do it. We have a right to do it, just because we can.

Many people we admire agree with the snake: They argue that any restrictions on human behavior encourage ignorance, tyranny, and the death of all serious inquiry. License and freedom are the same.

Let's look a little bit at the story. God has said, according to the woman in her conversation with the serpent, "Don't touch or eat of the tree in the middle of the garden or you shall die." Adam and Eve seem okay complying with God's request; a minimal discipline from every point of view—everything else in the GOE is fair game.

Along comes Mr. Snake. Here's his line:

"Hahahahaha! God has made that request so that you'll be stupid and ignorant and easy to manipulate! That tree has great tasting fruit! You eat; you not only have something tasty, you know good and evil just like God!"

Adam and Eve have not a clue what "knowing good and evil" means, but it sounds good and the fruit is pretty, so why not.

BAM!! What do they learn? They learn they are naked and have no clothes so they make some out of leaves. They learn to be ashamed, to feel bad about themselves. Not much "knowledge of good" in that. The snake has sold them a false package. It has only one ingredient, not two. Only knowledge of evil, no knowledge of good. Because guess what: knowledge of good is what they already had.

The Garden is a holy place. It is still available for us. An angel stands at the gate, yes, to keep us out if we are unwilling to sacrifice our knowledge of evil, our shame, our relentless feeling bad about ourselves.

But, if we are willing to live under the same discipline as was originally asked, if we are willing to eat of every fruit except that of the tree in the middle of the garden, then we are welcome, as we always have been. And we can live with the knowledge of good alone, unashamed and free once more.

Growing Where You Are Planted

Growing where you are planted is just fine, spiritually. You let good roots sink into your faith system, religious or secular, and you grow up into the plant you are created to be. Sometimes you grow fast, sometimes you grow slow, some seasons you don't grow at all.

Growing in place is not attractive to many people, spiritually. Their faith system is dead and meaningless to them except for a feature here or there. Or it's off on a detour route that makes no sense to you. No excitement, no joy, just silliness or nothing real.

People start to look around, spiritually. The Christian looker takes a peek at all sorts of things: Buddhism looks good—quiet, clean, "spiritual." Hinduism is colorful and fantastic, with tens of thousands of gods available to hear the slightest prayer. Judaism is strange and hard, Islam is scary but powerful, Fundamentalism of any stripe is also scary.

Other faiths are too obscure for major consideration.

What is wrong with looking around, spiritually? Not much, unless you are looking to uproot and be planted elsewhere. In fact, if you stick with your faith tradition and commit to growing in its soil, looking around is glorious and nurturing—you hear God in a million different ways, and this is fabulous fertilizer for your maturing spirit.

Transplanting is difficult, spiritually. You have grown up in a specific environment, religious, secular, both. You are more difficult to uproot and replant than you might think. Faith is a deeply sturdy plant, wherever it grows, but very often it languishes when transplanted to a different environment. The soil is different even if the water and the air are the same.

How to be a healthy plant, spiritually. Bring your spirit back to where you are planted and grow there. This may be heartbreaking news to some, but it is the healthy thing to do. Your faith may embarrass you and let you down. But stay there. Grow there. Let your roots sink, your branches grow. Learn from the other faiths you find so beautiful and apply their beauty to your own. But don't bolt the garden, or try to; you will weaken your plant, not strengthen it.

The healthy Christian plant, the healthy Buddhist plant, the healthy Jewish plant, and the healthy Muslim plant have more in common than any attempted grafts and transplants. They grow great! They all require discipline and attention, but in their own soils they root, grow, mature and propagate with less fatiguing rigor than required in different soil.

They share their joy in health, in relationship with God, in celebration of the earth, themselves and one another. Nobody is right and nobody is wrong; they are all just plants—God's holy jewels filling the garden with color, difference, and always joy.

Gladness

Gladness is a lovely feature of human life. It is a happy response of the soul to life as it is best lived. We are glad when we have friends, we are glad when a baby smiles, we are glad when we accomplish something important to us. It is a soft response and a beautiful one. It's not all that intense or focused, it is diffuse and peaceful.

Sometimes we use the word glad to mean less-than-honorable responses: I'm glad they're dead/going to prison/shut out of life some way. This isn't really "glad," it's a way of separating ourselves from fearful people who have done or we believe can do us harm, hurt us. It is in the vengeance spectrum, not the gladness spectrum. These are very different; we know that in our bones.

Sometimes we use the word glad to mean relief: I'm glad that test is over, the bills got addressed as best as possible, the cleaning got started, and the laundry got done (and put away)! But gladness is different from relief. Gladness is about the present. We are relieved a stressful task is done; we are glad we can enjoy clean clothes and the way they smell and feel.

Where is God in all this? Right with us! God is God of the present—that is where we know God best, most personally. If you are glad, God is right there. Well, God is right there whether you are hurt, afraid and vengeful or whether you are stressed and relieved. But we are freer to appreciate and experience God when we are glad. There is no ego in gladness, there are no walls either up or tumbling down, there is just the gladness, our soul's happy response to life this moment.

We all know people who are rarely glad. These beloved creatures of God are trapped in anticipation of the future (which never happens correctly) or in past assaults that never get shed, healed or forgiven. They are so terrified of the present, of something horrible happening—right now—that they can't see a pretty smile, a lovely flower, a lazy day. It is the job of those of us who are glad, who are free enough to know gladness, to hold these injured souls in our gladness.

What does this mean? It does not mean that we say, "Hey look, there's a lovely flower! Let's be glad about it!" It means that we, glad because of the lovely flower, reach out and hold that damaged person in our glad hearts. It means we hear all the fear and acrimony they lay on us. It means we, out of the gladness of our hearts, minister to the truly unlovely, the hardest to love of all human beings: the ones who can never be glad.

Gladness: a lovely, peaceful, pleasant state known in the moment, in the present. We can access gladness simply by being in the moment and letting our souls recognize the blessings God has set before us to delight our souls. Gladness; the soft light at night, the soft response to the day, the diffuse presence of God that never leaves, is always there.

I Know
How You Feel

Rule one, two, three, and on: Never say this.

You may think you're being helpful when you say this, but you are not. That comment, whether you are conscious of it or not, is not about the suffering person beside you, it is about you and what you know. The suffering person is with you because of vulnerable hopes that you will listen with your heart to the suffering and simply be there and care. The suffering person is not there to hear that—in your opinion—you've had a similar experience that qualifies you to be counted as caring.

The ONLY place where this comment might fit in is in groups where it is not necessary because it is known and foregone: alcoholics anonymous, mothers of suicide victims, etc.: very focused, very caring communities for very specific ailments, situations or tragedies, etc. And even there, what is shared is a common experience, not necessarily common feelings.

More evidence? The emotions ("feelings") are notoriously temperamental and even more notoriously special to each individual, especially in crisis. To say "I know how you feel" about something intensely personal and stressful to another individual is an assault, which they can't handle at the moment. You are assaulting the individuality of their emotions and the emotions do not like that at all. If you absolutely have to say "I know how you feel," to someone, please restrict the comment to things you know that the person doesn't care about or have any investment in: t-shirt color, sock style, or there's always the weather.

How do you communicate caring? By being there, with a hurt person. You don't have to speak your caring, you have to live it. You live it in person, on the phone, email, text, drum beat—whatever communication device is available. It is reassuring for a wounded person to know there is a stable full of people who care. It is healing. The lives in this stable may be called on only silently, only as part of the stable of carers. "I'm here," is all you ever have to say. The wounded person knows and is grateful.

And "I'm here," is what God says, too. Holy Companion. God is the wounded person's Holy Companion. You are, too, when you live "I'm here." When you reflect on your own wounded self, you see that this is true: "I'm here," is healing, is enough. No one needs to know how you feel; everyone needs to know you are "there," are "here." That is the holy support we give each other in sorrow and tragedy; the holy support we share with God.

Allowing God

Most of us who believe sort of or even greatly in a relationship with God, have a tendency to not let God participate in the relationship. We are happy to do things we think God would like, sing nice songs about God and give God thanks for this or that. But we rarely take time to allow God a real presence in our lives, time to be a powerful and immediate guide, partner, companion, back-up, spouse, etc. during the day and night.

God's "relationship" with us is something we hold largely theoretical: God Cares for Us. We've been taught that from the get-go. Must be true. Then off we go, doing good and helpful things, assuming God is pleased with them, and generally God is.

However, a rich and living relationship with anyone is more than a fairly decent report card of good works presented to another. If the sum total of your relationship with your parents or guardians was the relationship built around your report card, you would find that relationship missing something. You are missing something; the parents/guardians are missing something. There is more to be had.

What we need to do is allow God time for God's relationship with us. To only ask God for support with this, assistance with that, and so on is to have no relationship with your friends except when it comes to asking them to lend you a hand now and then. Generally they will do that, but the relationship is based on more.

How to do this with God? You allow God to relate to you, to be in the room with you, sit on the couch with you, be with you on a walk, and just be with you. Great relationships are based on people being together, existing in the same space, being aware of each other in real time, real places. We are poorly taught this; we are taught works and worship are sufficient—do good, go to church. But just being with God is most important of all, like just being with your kids, or best friend, or parents, or your pets. Just being together.

This takes practice, the practice of the presence of God, as Brother Lawrence would say. God is always with you, for sure, but the key to developing the relationship is being aware of it—that there are two of you in the room. You need to allow God to work God's part of the relationship—to be with you and share your life, little bits, and big ones.

And, so you know and live the relationship, you allow yourself to slowly develop an interest in God's life, to be part of it—supportive, loving, all the rest. This is a relationship, a relationship of allowing: allowing love between two holy beings to root, grow, blossom and entwine. Forever.

Inspiration

Swingin' Loose has come about because a good friend said this book would be a good thing to do and I believed him. So thank you, Charles D. Smith!

Writing

Jane Lee Wolfe works for women's rights and for spiritual health and fitness in the world. She was President of the World Young Women's Christian Association serving 25 million women. She is Director of Bog Chapel, Inc., serving anyone interested in getting their spiritual life in some kind of order. Let's hear it for me!

And let me hear from you:

> Bog Chapel, Inc.
> P.O. Box 5
> Woodstock, VT 05091
> info@bogchapel.org

.S

CPSIA information can be obtained at www.ICGtesting.com
Printed in the USA
BVOW06s2241061013

332784BV00001B/3/P